If There's ANYTHING I Can Do

WHAT YOU *Can* DO WHEN SERIOUS ILLNESS STRIKES

BY JOSEPHINE H. HICKS

To ABJ

Praise for "If There's Anything I Can Do…"

"A down to earth and eminently practical guide for anyone affected by serious illness — I wish I'd had this resource when I served as a hospice chaplain. Think of this book as a bird sitting on your shoulder, reminding you to pay attention to what the patient and family say (and don't say), to listen deeply to your own responses, and to act in the most helpful and loving ways possible."

— The Most Rev. Dr. Katharine Jefferts Schori,
Presiding Bishop of The Episcopal Church

"Maori people have a wonderful saying, 'ahakoa iti, he pounamu'. Literally translated the words mean that although what is being gifted maybe small, it is nonetheless as incalculably precious as is pounamu more commonly known as priceless jade or greenstone.

Josephine Hicks here offers If There's Anything I Can Do, as her small but incalculably precious literary gift of gentle reflective wisdom and of wise practical advice to those often so unexpectedly called to be care-givers of loved ones.

A wonderful pastoral care resource book, which deftly and yet sensitively displaces those understandable but often ultimately unhelpful human responses to personal crisis, such as helplessness, anger or avoidance. Instead we are here offered a superb inventory of pragmatic tips and techniques intended to enable both those called to the sacred task of care-giving as well as those challenged by serious illness into unplanned dependency, to negotiate for best ways of together reconciling the extreme joys, the unbearable sadnesses and the interminably ordinary things that inevitably arise in the process of seeking to live fully and with grace into the end times of those we love, often so utterly inexpressibly…"

— Dr. Jenny Te Paa, Dean of the School of Theology, College of St John The Evangelist, Auckland, New Zealand

"As a hospital chaplain, I daily encounter patients and caregivers walking the difficult journey of serious illness. Often, patients and caregivers are in desperate need of support, but are too overwhelmed to articulate their needs, and friends who long to help do not know what words or actions will be helpful. If There's Anything I Can Do *is an ideal guide; honest, clear and heartfelt, it offers practical ways to give and receive love and support amidst the confusion and pain that serious illness brings. A must read for patients, their caregivers and the friends and family who love them. This practical, experience-based book is just what is needed when patients and caregivers wonder: "what do I need?" and when their friends ask "how can I help?"*

— The Rev. Elizabeth Welch, MDiv, BCC
Sojourn Chaplaincy at San Francisco General Hospital

"Insightful, accurate, precise, and free of fluff, If There's Anything I Can Do *should be required reading for caregivers, patients and healthcare workers. As an oncologist, I'm glad to have this resource for my patients and their families. As the husband of a recently diagnosed cancer patient, I'm grateful someone else has gone through this and can tell me what to expect."*

— David W. Miller, M.D.

"This one of the most helpful pastoral resources I've come across in a long time. Clergy and friends who want to help anyone facing serious illness will find it a tremendously helpful guide — both on a profound and practical level — on how to care for others when words fail."

— The Rt Rev. Stacy Sauls, Bishop of
the Episcopal Diocese of Lexington

"This resource reminds us of the support needed by all families facing end-of-life and other critical care situations and gives guidance on how to offer support that makes a real difference. This book adds to the growing number of resources available to patients and families to help them through this critical time. The experiences shared also show that hospice is a true resource for all involved in end-of-life events."

— Galen Miller, Executive Vice President
National Hospice & Palliative Care Organization

"Many of us, and, in fact, almost all women, will be family caregivers to loved ones experiencing serious illness and needing care at life's end. Yet, as a society, we provide almost no physical, emotional, financial or spiritual support for those who do this vital work. Josephine Hicks' wonderful little book, If There's Anything I Can Do…What You Can Do when Serious Illness Strikes, *is born out of lived experience of loving care giving for her partner as she journeyed through the end of life. It contains wonderful gems of wisdom and practical tips for all of us to learn and heed as we attempt to support caregivers. I particularly loved her "lessons learned" summaries at the end of each chapter, especially in the chapter "If You're Inclined To Say This, Don't." Josephine is a fountain of short, pithy pearls of wisdom and advice for those of us who often so inadequately attempt to find words and deeds to support our friends and family who are doing the work of care giving. I highly recommend it."*

— Richard Payne, MD
Professor of Medicine and Divinity
Esther Colliflower Director
Duke Institute on Care at the End of Life

TABLE OF CONTENTS

INTRODUCTION

ANN **B**REWSTER **J**ONES, my partner of 17 years, died on February 28, 2010 of pancreatic cancer at the all-too-early age of 57. She was diagnosed in April 2006. That diagnosis thrust us into the world of life with cancer. Ann's path included surgery, chemotherapy, radiation, remission, a new tumor, more radiation, remission, and ultimate recurrence with no hope of treatment, only palliative care. The initial surgery was a lengthy and complicated procedure. She was in the hospital 28 days, followed by a slow recuperation at home, as we tried to get her body strong enough to take on the chemotherapy. Complications over the years led to more hospitalizations. She lived almost four years after her diagnosis — virtually unheard of with pancreatic cancer. At the end she was in a residential Hospice facility for a month, again exceeding all predictions as her body hung on longer than anyone anticipated.

I shouldn't have been surprised that Ann would defy all predictions concerning her death. She defied the odds in her life as well. She went to The Episcopal Church's Virginia Theological Seminary in 1974, before the Church decided to ordain women as priests. That decision came during her time at seminary. Later she became the first woman parish rector[1] in the Diocese of Missouri.

[1] The head clergy person in a parish in The Episcopal Church is called the "rector."

Ann and I met at the church she came to serve in Charlotte, North Carolina in 1992. We quickly realized how much we enjoyed being together — whether on a hike, at a movie, or roaming around a bookstore. She liked watching me coach little league softball, coming to watch me encourage the girls even though she was the only non-parent in the bleachers. I loved how she could engage anybody — and I mean anybody — in an interesting conversation. She learned the life story of a park ranger in Glacier National Park while he was helping us retrieve keys I had locked in our rental car. She engaged each and every nurse and nurse's aide during four years of treatments in discussions about healthcare, nursing education, and their lives.

The Church was an important part of our lives together. I loved that she was a priest in the Church I love so much. I'll never forget the gleam in her eye as she announced to our congregation that I had been elected to the Executive Council (akin to the national board of directors) of The Episcopal Church.

Ann enjoyed learning new things. She wanted to learn about Twitter in the late stages of her disease. Sadly, a cruel complication of Ann's cancer caused her to lose the ability to find the words she wanted and made it difficult for her to communicate in her last months. The intellect came through nonetheless. Once when I was struggling to understand what she was trying to tell me she got frustrated and said, "Why are you being so obtuse?" She couldn't find the basic word she was looking for, but "obtuse" was on the tip of her tongue.

In the months of Ann's remission, we enjoyed some glorious times. We went to Canada and got married. We took a cruise on a small ship in Alaska. The "everyday" became treasured times with friends and with each other — relaxing meals, walks in the neighborhood, Scrabble games, movies…life.

At one point, a new dress was the most exciting thing. Ann had feared the worst from the day she was diagnosed. For many months she was unwilling to plan for anything that would occur more than a few weeks away. Then one day she met me at the door with a huge grin as she said: "Let me show you my new dress." This was not just any dress. She bought it to wear at a glamorous dance to honor her daughter. I was thrilled — not just about the dress, but because the dance was six months away. She was planning for something in the future!

Ann was not content to sit idly during her remission, even if she wasn't strong enough to work full time. She took piano lessons, returning to an old love. She volunteered at the Humane Society. She found her niche as a "cat cuddler." (I'm not making that up. Her title was "cat cuddler.") Her job was to socialize cats so that they would be more attractive candidates for adoption. Ann lectured the cats regularly. If they hissed, she admonished them: "You will never be adopted if you hiss." Encouraging better behavior, she instructed them that they must purr when being held.

Ann was not always a strict instructor, however. The best part of the day for Ann was when the little boy next door came home from daycare. He toddled around from the car and up our walkway to the front door. He pressed his face against the lowest window panes in the door and called "Ann?" She greeted him at the door with "Miracle Bubbles" for him to wave around the lawn. They talked and laughed and took short walks. They loved life together during those twilight moments.

Ann never lost her deeply caring nature. It was never about her, even as she faced terminal illness and horrific treatments. Only two months post-surgery, and in the midst of chemo treatments, Ann worried that my birthday would be lost in the shuffle. She e-mailed my friends and asked everyone to send me a card. She intercepted them as they came in the mail. On my birthday, she presented me with an amazing stack of cards with wonderful notes from friends far and wide.

Perhaps the most treasured "normal" moment with Ann happened on Christmas Eve 2009, just two months before she died. I took Ann shopping, in a wheelchair, so that she could buy Christmas gifts. After she made her purchases, I wheeled her around the mall to see the store windows. We were then enjoying a cup of coffee when she looked at me and said: "I just like doing things with you. We discovered that early on." So true. On that day, just being with her was the greatest Christmas gift ever.

"Small tokens of sincere consideration or love carry messages far beyond their size."
— KARL-HANS VON FREMDE

CHAPTER 1

"If There's Anything I Can Do"

THROUGH THE YEARS OF ANN'S DISEASE, our friends and families were wonderfully supportive. Everyone wanted to help us in any way they could. Many knew exactly what to do. Others struggled, not knowing what to do.

I found myself hearing, many times a day: "If there's anything I can do…." Sometimes the exchange went on and on, as the person who wanted to console me frankly didn't know what to say or do. So she kept saying: "Really. Anything. If there's anything I can do." I engaged in this uncomfortable dance with well-meaning people for four years.

The problem, of course, is that few know what to say or do. In a sense, there isn't anything any of us can do to address the real issue. None of us can make the disease go away. None of us can bring the person back from the dead. We feel utterly helpless because we are. We fall back on the only thing we can think of to say: "If there's anything I can do…."

I don't have any magic answers. But I do have some thoughts. I have had a few years of experience as a caregiver and a recent experience of the death of a spouse after a lengthy dying process.

I am not a social scientist. I have not researched any of this. I have no training in medicine or psychology. I have talked with friends who have faced cancer. One of Ann's closest friends, John, was diagnosed with head and neck cancer a year after Ann was diagnosed. Another friend, Joe, went through lengthy treatments for melanoma during Ann's illness. My law partner Heloise helped her husband through brain cancer. Neighbor and friend Tim faced every treatment imaginable for colon cancer that metastasized to his liver. He and his wife Laurie accompanied us on many walks in the neighborhood, in support group meetings, and in the unwelcome walk that is life with cancer.

I have consulted with a counselor who has over 20 years' experience in counseling cancer patients and their families and helping them navigate the overwhelming and stormy waters they have been thrust into. I have heard many stories from patients and caregivers I have met along the way, some of whom are referred to in these pages. Mostly, however, what I offer here is based on my experience and my observations. I hope to give you some insights on things that can be remarkably helpful and things that tend not to be helpful. I will try to impart a few helpful hints if not words of wisdom by telling you a few stories and leaving you with a few suggestions.

For those of you who want to cut to the chase (after all, there are sick and suffering who need your help and you now want to avoid at all costs saying "If there's anything I can do…") here it is. Bottom line: *Just do it.*

Asking someone what you can do puts the burden on them to articulate what they need. People who are hurting may not even know what they need. No matter how much you emphasize the word "anything" — with a press of the arm or super sincere voice or a flashing neon sign (isn't there an app for that now?) — the person you want to help doesn't want to impose on you and doesn't know what is fair to ask of you. We had a long list of people eager to help — with "anything" — but when we actually needed something, Ann would be reluctant to burden anyone. She would say, "She has young children," or "She works full time," or "He lives all the way across town."

NOTE TO PATIENTS AND CAREGIVERS

"Hear the heart." Hear that people care about you, even if they are saying something that sounds inept or is not helpful. They don't know what to say or how to say it. They are uncomfortable with your pain and your disease. They want to do the right thing but have no idea how. It is literally impossible for them to truly know what you are feeling and what you are going through. They are doing the best they can. They mean well. Be patient with them.

Think of something you think would be helpful (after you read this I hope you'll have lots of ideas) and think of something that will be easy for you. What do you have the skill, the time, and the inclination to do? Do you like to cook? Do you have time to sit with the patient or run errands? Can you take care of the dog or the children? If you make it relatively easy on yourself, it will be easier for everyone. It will seem less of a burden on you and will seem less of an imposition to the patient and caregiver.

The good news is that many of the most helpful things you can do are small things. A wise person once said: "Great opportunities to help others seldom come, but small ones surround us every day."[2]

Don't worry that you don't know what to do or can't possibly do anything grand enough to truly help. Just do what you can. It will make a big difference.

Finally, don't be offended or hurt if it isn't the perfect thing at the moment or if the patient or caregiver turns you down. Know that offering is appreciated, and offering something or doing something concrete is eminently preferable to saying "Let me know what I can do."

One caveat before you read any further: These musings are based on my experience and my reactions, or my partner's reactions. Cancer and serious health conditions are intensely personal experiences. Not everyone will have the same reactions we did. Many

[2] Sally Koch

of the thoughts expressed in these pages seem to be widely held views among the cancer patients and caregivers I know. Needless to say, however, tailor any thoughts here to your own experience and your own understanding of the person you want to help.

"It is not so much our friends' help that helps us as the confidence of their help."

— EPICURUS

"The minute you think you've got it made, disaster is just around the corner."

— JOE PATERNO

CHAPTER 2

The Day the Outside Came In

IN **1989,** Hurricane Hugo hit Charlotte, North Carolina, with full force. Any time a hurricane hits land it is devastating. When a hurricane hits 200 miles inland, it is other-worldly.

Charlotte is known as a city of trees. Many neighborhood streets are lined with enormous ancient oaks, whose trunks are Sequoia-esque and whose limbs cover streets and lawns with a beautiful, wide canopy. Hurricane Hugo snapped hundred-year old oaks like twigs, smashing cars and houses and leaving a snarl of wreckage in its wake. It blew out huge electrical transformers all over town, creating an eerie "fireworks" display through the dark hours of the night and leaving thousands of residents and businesses without power for eighteen days. The National Guard came in to prevent looting and help the city begin to dig out from the devastation.

One of the enormous trees landed not only on my friend Karen's house but actually split the roof open and landed *in* her house. It fell on her, pinning her down for an excruciating two hours. Her husband couldn't even begin to lift a tree the size of a stretch Hummer. Eventually she was extricated and taken to the hospital to begin the long road of surgeries and rehabilitation.

For years her son, who was four at the time, referred to that day as *"the day the outside came in."*

Cancer is like that. Heart attacks are like that. All tragedy is like that. Hurricanes are not supposed to hit 200 miles inland. Trees are not supposed to fall on people inside houses. Cancer and heart attacks and tragedy are things that happen to other people. Things I read about in the newspaper or hear about at book club. Not things that happen to me or the people I love.

April 20, 2006, was the day the outside came in for me.

Ann called me at work and said tearfully, "I have a tumor on my pancreas."

What? I knew she had been having gastro-intestinal issues, but a *tumor?* Okay, okay, she had had an intensely painful attack in the middle of the night a few weeks before, but a *tumor?* Seriously?

I sat at my desk at work in a daze, not knowing what to think or do. Could this really be happening to us? "Okay," I rationalized. "We don't know yet exactly what this means. We don't even know if it is cancer. And even if it is, cancer isn't the automatic death sentence it once was — *right? Someone please tell me that's right!"* For the next few days, we couldn't bring ourselves to use the "C" word. After all, the doctors didn't know if it was a *malignant* tumor. They weren't calling it *"cancer,"* at least not yet. So we kept calling it a tumor. But a tumor is scary enough. No one who is this close to me is supposed to have a tumor. Hurricanes aren't supposed to hit 200 miles inland. Trees aren't supposed to fall inside your house. But for us, the outside had come crashing in.

*"Life changes in the instant.
The ordinary instant."*
— JOAN DIDION
(THE YEAR OF MAGICAL THINKING)

"The single biggest problem in communication is the illusion that it has taken place."

— George Bernard Shaw

CHAPTER 3

What We [Don't Want to] Have Here is a Failure to Communicate

WE HAD TEN DAYS between the time we learned Ann had a tumor and the day of her surgery. We were told to expect her to be in the hospital eight to ten days and then have a slow recuperation at home. We knew chemotherapy and radiation would likely follow. I felt completely overwhelmed with the diagnosis and with a "to do" list that seemed endless.

A friend called during that time and told me about a website called CaringBridge, a free on-line community for people who are seriously ill, their friends and family.

When she told me about it I said, "That sounds great but I really cannot handle one more thing on my 'to do' list."

She said, "Not to worry. I'll set it up for you and we will post the updates if you want."

She set it up, and for days all I had to do was call her or her partner with updates. They posted them on the website for me. It was terrific. Eventually I wrote the updates, and later still Ann wrote her own updates.

Here is what makes CaringBridge terrific: You only have to write your update once, and you can read people's responses when you are ready to read them. It is infinitely better than fielding telephone calls. (*Will the blasted phone ever stop ringing? I'm on the verge of ripping the cord from the wall and throwing my cell phone out of the window.*) It is even better than endless e-mails in your in box. CaringBridge is just there when you need and want to see supportive messages.

You can post photographs as well as messages. People can log in whenever and wherever they want to check on the status. They can also sign up for an e-mail notice whenever you update the site. Our friends really appreciated this site. One friend was traveling shortly after Ann's surgery and was eager for news. She wrote, "Greetings from Budapest. My first stop on arrival was to check your site and find out how you are doing." Another wrote: "It is nice to know your friends can communicate with you without having to invade your room!"

The notes to Ann varied from prayerful support to light-hearted fun. Ann's surgery was on May 1. One friend wrote: "I'll be thinking of you as I march through Red Square on May Day. May the masses rise up in support of a great mother of the revolution."

Another who was struck by how many people had

sent messages of support so quickly wrote: "General Custer may have survived Little Big Horn if he had but a fraction of the wagons encircling him as you do."

Many were quick notes: "Thinking of you." Don't worry about making your note profound or "deep." The text is less important than the fact that you reached out. Ann was more interested many times in who had written a note than in hearing what the note said.

We loved getting notes on this site. And I now have a history of our story, told through the postings on this

NOTE TO PATIENTS AND CAREGIVERS

A few words to the wise about sending updates. First, recognize that people are hungry for news about you. They are worried about you and want to know how things are going. Post updates periodically. Have a friend send updates for you if it is too much for you to do. Second, be careful what you report and how you report it. I tended to put a positive spin on how things were going for Ann, even when she was having a pretty rough time in the hospital. People then naturally responded with remarks like: "I'm glad it is going so well." Ann was not happy. "What are you telling people? It is not going well," she cried. Ann wanted people to understand how sick she was. She was disappointed when it seemed as if people weren't getting that message. Try to be accurate in your reporting.

site, along with all of the wonderful, encouraging notes we got along the way.

Finally, if you are writing a note to the patient, acknowledge how tough it is when things are indeed tough. No matter what we reported, people invariably picked up on and commented on any positive thing they could find to remark on. That's understandable. People want to focus on the positive. It is uncomfortable and awkward to focus on the negative. But for the person who is going through a hard time, it feels as if people don't get it when they send positive notes that ignore the painful, the frustrating, the frightening, and the uncertain realities the patient and her family are going through. Try to acknowledge those things in your notes to them.

Bottom line: communication is important — to and from the patient and caregiver on the one hand and friends and family on the other. CaringBridge, or a site like it, is one great avenue but by no means the only one. Read on. The next section — "Don't Call Us, We'll Call You"— has more suggestions on communication.

LESSONS LEARNED

■ Let the patient and her family control the information flow; don't call them for updates.

■ If the family hasn't set up a CaringBridge site or a similar web site, offer to do it for them. If they don't want to use a web site, offer to help set up a blog or send out e-mails or make calls to report updates to friends and family.

■ Be sensitive to what the patient and her family are telling you, and be as supportive as you can while acknowledging the gravity or difficulty of what the patient and her family are going through.

■ The text of your message is less important sometimes than the fact that you reached out. A short message may be perfect. You don't have to be profound. Just be yourself.

*"All phone calls
are obscene."*

— Karen Elizabeth Gordon

CHAPTER 4

Don't Call Us, We'll Call You

"**IF THAT PHONE RINGS ONE MORE TIME...,**" one of us said routinely. The phone in the hospital room. The cell phones. The phone at the house. It seemed relentless. It sounded jarring. It woke Ann up. It concerned us that doctors or nurses or pharmacies who really needed to reach us would get a busy signal and not be able to call back soon enough. It was one more call for us to answer and respond to — or to ignore, knowing we would have to return the call later. In the last several months we finally turned off the ringer on every phone in the house to avoid hearing the phone ring.

Of course you want to know how things are going or how you can help. You want to hear the patient's voice. You have nothing but the family's best interests at heart, and they will understand. All of that is true.

But here is the best piece of advice I can give you: *When someone you love is in crisis, try to remember it is not about you*. It is not about what you want or need. It is about what will make the patient and caregiver's life easier and let them know that you care, without adding to their burden or stress.

We loved hearing from friends and family, especially in a way that let us get the message and respond (a) only if we felt we wanted to and (b) when we had the time and energy to devote to it.

Cards are always welcome. One friend sent Ann a post card every day while she was in the hospital. It usually had only a line or two in it, but it brightened her day and let her know this friend was thinking about her every day. Everyone loves getting cards in the mail. Cards, notes, letters, and messages on a web site like CaringBridge all have the advantage of being there when the patient and caregiver want to read them. E-mails are less intrusive than phone calls. Even a text message can be preferable to a phone call, because it doesn't have to be answered right away.

One of the greatest gifts you can give the patient and caregiver is to make clear that you do not expect or need a response to your message or call. Our friend Joe endured lengthy treatments for melanoma. He was grateful for friends who cared and wanted to help, but keeping up with all of the calls and messages was exhausting. It felt like a full time job. He was greatly relieved to get a card that he could read when he wanted and didn't need a reply.

One more point on this topic, on the "we'll call you" side of the adage: If the patient or caregiver calls you to ask for something, recognize that there is likely desperation behind the call. There may or may not be desperation in his or her voice, but don't let that fool you.

I have fumbled the ball badly on this front myself. I told a friend whose husband had just been diagnosed with cancer to call me any time, day or night, if I could help or if she just wanted to talk. I gave her every telephone number where she could reach me. One night as I sat down to dinner at a restaurant with friends, she called. I told her I was out with friends and asked if I could call her back. She of course said that was fine, and we did talk as soon as I finished dinner. But I had let her down. I should have taken her call, excusing myself from the table for a few minutes to talk to her. All I needed to do was take the time to listen to her, when she needed me, not when it suited me.

Marlene Dietrich once said: "It's the friends you can call up at 4:00 a.m. who matter." How true. If you offer to be one of those friends, be prepared to follow through.

LESSONS LEARNED

- Avoid calling the patient or caregiver.

- Use CaringBridge or a similar web site or e-mails or blogs to let the family control the flow of information about how things are going and what they need.

- If you want to contact the patient or family, use a card, a note, CaringBridge, an e-mail, or a text message — something that will not disturb them and that they can respond to when it suits them.

- Unless you truly need a reply, make clear that you do not expect a reply to your e-mail or text.

- If you can't refrain from calling, and you get voice

mail, leave a short message so that the patient can hear your voice, but make clear that you don't need a call back.

■ If the patient or caregiver calls you, recognize the likely desperation behind the call. Be ready to listen and do whatever you can to help, right then.

"It's the friends you can call up at 4:00 a.m. who matter."

— MARLENE DIETRICH

"Animals are such agreeable friends — they ask no questions, they pass no criticisms."

— GEORGE ELIOT

CHAPTER 5

P.A.W.S. (Pets Are Wonderful Support)[1]

ANN AND I HAD A DOG AND A CAT when Ann was diagnosed. Initially, I hadn't thought about needing help with either one. Thankfully for me, a wonderful colleague was two steps ahead of me.

As I was frantically trying to get things in the office squared away to allow me to be out for a few weeks, a young woman in my group came to see me. She said, "I'm so sorry about Ann. I live in your neighborhood and have a dog and a dog walker who comes every day. I'd be happy to take care of your dog while Ann is in the hospital."

I had not even had time to think about what to do with the dog or that I needed to do anything about the dog, and here a solution had been dropped into my lap. My dog not only stayed at her house, but she arranged for someone else to take the dog when she had to go out of town and Ann's hospital stay lasted

---

[1] A terrific organization in Los Angeles and San Francisco calls itself P.A.W.S., which stands for Pets Are Wonderful Support. P.A.W.S. recognizes how important animals can be as companions for HIV/AIDS patients. Pets are indeed wonderful support, but they also need to be taken care of. That is part of P.A.W.S.' mission — to help provide vet care, pet food, dog walking, grooming, and other services to allow low income HIV/AIDS patients to keep their pets.

much longer than we had anticipated. She always let me know where the dog was, but I never had to worry about it. It was enormously helpful.

Once the CaringBridge site got going, one of our friends wrote early on that she would be happy to do anything for us, even clean out the kitty litter. Other friends picked up on that, many offering to clean out the kitty litter and others offering to do anything but. It became a running joke. Ann finally wrote a CaringBridge entry saying she was surprised to learn that her friends fell into two categories — those who change kitty litter and those who don't.

When Ann was in the hospital, she got a visit that cheered her up more than either of us would have imagined. Ann always loved to explain: "I am not a dog person. I am a person who owns a dog." So I wasn't expecting her to be particularly excited when Molly, a Miniature Schnauzer, walked into her hospital room. Molly got up on Ann's bed, licked her face, and sat in her lap. Ann loved it. She told me it was the most "human" she had felt since she was admitted to the hospital.

Much later, when Ann was bedridden and I was juggling in-home nurses with my own schedule, our neighbor Eleanor noticed our cat was limping. She brought the cat to the door and offered to take her to the vet. I was not happy about having another "patient" in the house but was grateful for the offer of help. Eleanor took the cat to the vet, got the medicine and instructions we needed to take care of her, and returned her safe and sound. It was such a huge help.

LESSONS LEARNED

- Make it easy for the patient and caregiver. When my colleague offered to take care of the dog, all I had to do was take my dog to her house, which was close by. She took care of the rest.

- Does the patient have a dog or pet? Offer to take care of it, if you can, or find someone who can, while they are in the hospital. If they are home, offer to walk the dog, change the kitty litter, or pick up pet supplies — anything that lets the pet be a companion and not a burden.

- Do you have a dog that would be good around patients and hospitals? If so, volunteer to take your dog to visit patients. It is wonderfully uplifting for patients.

"Tenterhooks are the upholstery of the anxious seat."
— ROBERT SHERWOOD

CHAPTER 6

"Take a Seat. We'll Let You Know When You Can See Her."

CAREGIVERS AND FAMILY MEMBERS spend a lot of time in waiting rooms. Waiting while the patient is in surgery. Waiting while the patient is getting a scan. Waiting while the patient is getting a chemotherapy treatment. Waiting for the doctor to make her rounds. Caregivers grow accustomed to hearing: "Take a seat. We'll let you know when you can see her (or when you can take her home)."

My friend Heloise's husband had been through surgery, scans, and treatments to attack his brain tumor. She knew I was facing a lot of anxious time in waiting rooms.

The day before we took Ann to the hospital for her surgery, I found a care package from Heloise on our front porch. It was full of puzzle books, pencils, magazines she knew I would like — light, entertaining, distracting material that did not require a lot of concentration or focused time. She knew that time in waiting rooms and in hospital rooms is frequently interrupted. You may think you will have time for the novel you've been meaning to read, but you will be too distracted to concentrate on it. The puzzles and magazines were perfect. We kept them in the hospital room for anyone who sat with Ann. It was a small gift, but a huge help.

Other friends agreed to sit with me during Ann's surgery. We knew it would likely last six to eight hours. There aren't enough puzzles or books to get some people through that many anxious hours. Different friends came and sat for a while. One brought lunch. Another said a prayer. Most just sat and talked about anything and nothing. It was very comforting and helped me get through the day. It was also a great comfort to Ann to know that I had support and was not sitting alone in the waiting room.

Not everyone will want company, however. Some caregivers would rather be left alone to their own thoughts or a distracting book. Making conversation with even a close friend may feel burdensome. Let the caregiver do what is best for her. If you haven't been asked to sit with her in the waiting room, that may be a sign that she doesn't want company. If you offer to sit with her, let her know you will not be offended if she would rather be alone.

LESSONS LEARNED

- If you think the caregiver would like company, offer to sit with her during surgery or lengthy procedures — or just show up, with a cup of coffee or just a smile.

- If the caregiver prefers not to have company, respect that. She may need that time for herself.

- Drop off a care package with puzzle books, pencils, and light reading the caregiver will enjoy.

"Worries go down better with soup than without."

— YIDDISH PROVERB

CHAPTER 7

Food Glorious Food

SOUTHERNERS KNOW HOW TO RESPOND TO CRISIS. It's called a casserole.

Food is a universal issue for any family that has someone in the hospital or someone at home recuperating. Meals can also be an easy way to help. But even accepting gifts of food can present challenges.

Several of the saints who came to my rescue over the different phases when we needed food offered to coordinate meals for me. These Foodie Saints contacted people, set up a schedule, gave instructions on when and where to deliver meals, and gave guidance on what to bring and what not to bring. That was a huge gift to me — one less call to make or field each day, and one less thing to worry about.

One of these Foodie Saints also went above and beyond the coordination of meals. She stopped by our house on her way home from work each day while Ann was in the hospital. She brought in the mail, took the food delivered that day to the refrigerator, threw out anything I hadn't had a chance to eat that had gotten old, fed the cat, and generally checked on things. It was enormously helpful. It allowed me, when I took a short break from the hospital, to take care of myself (take a shower, eat a relaxed meal, take a deep breath) rather than having to take care of things at the house.

We got better at this after learning some lessons when Ann was in the hospital during that month-long stretch. We realized that daily deliveries of food were too much for us. This happened in part because people tended to send huge portions, and in part because even smaller portions added up when we were out of the house for so long. We eventually settled on having meals delivered twice a week, which gave us just enough leftovers to tide us over and did not overwhelm us. We also asked people not to send more than enough for three to four servings.

The food was certainly welcome. Many a day I found myself harried, exasperated, exhausted, worried…when suddenly the door bell rang and there stood a friend with a smile and a hot, home-cooked meal ready for us to eat. Truly heaven sent.

I recently learned about a web site that I did not know about when we needed meals, but it looks helpful: www.mealbaby.com. It essentially takes the role of a meal coordinator. You create a page friends can log onto and see your food preferences and a calendar of dates to sign up for meals. You can see which dates are open and which are covered. The family can log on and see from whom to expect a delivery and when. It also lists near-by restaurants where the family could use gift cards. My friends realized that those gift cards could come in handy, and I appreciated having take-out options as well as home cooked meals.

Here's another example of how to make it easy for the family: One afternoon a friend called and said, "I am on my way to the Fresh Market to pick up something for dinner. What can I pick up for you?" She then listed wonderful-sounding prepared foods she was offering to deliver to my door. I jumped at the offer, and we had several delicious meals from that delivery. The key is that *she made it easy for me and made it clear that it was easy for her*. It did not take her out of her way or add to her "to do" list for the day.

A neighbor did a similarly wonderful thing when she told me, "I have a teenage son. I am at the grocery store practically every day. Please let me know if I can pick something up for you." I took her up on it the day Ann came home from the hospital. I called, and lo and behold, she was at the grocery store at that very moment. She picked up some things we needed and dropped them off twenty minutes later. Again, this was something that did not require her to go out of her way or add anything burdensome to her list, which made it easier for me to take her up on the offer.

Food for the caregiver in the hospital is another seemingly small thing that can be fraught with stress. Eating in the hospital room is a juggling exercise, in every respect — literally juggling food on your lap while jumping up every few minutes to take care of something the patient needs, and figuratively juggling your own need for fuel with all of the other demands on your time. Every day brings a new judgment call. Should I take the time to take a shower or to eat a meal outside of the hospital? Wolfing down hospital cafeteria food too often becomes the default.

Encourage the caregiver to go out for a meal. Offer to sit with the patient while the caregiver enjoys a little break over a meal. If she needs to stay close by, offer to eat in the cafeteria with her. Company and conversation about something other than the next round of meds may be welcome.

Surprisingly, however, one of the best meals I have ever eaten was actually in the hospital room. A friend called me late one Saturday afternoon while Ann was in the hospital and said "Meet me at the entrance. I just grilled some steaks and have a plate for you." Steak and baked potato never tasted so good, before or since.

LESSONS LEARNED

■ Have a single point person coordinate meals, taking that burden off of the caregiver.

■ Set up a web site at mealbaby.com or lotsahelpinghands.com. Both of these web sites include calendars. Mealbaby.com has a calendar showing when meals need to be delivered. Lotsahelpinghands.com has a calendar of activities and family needs, including meals or picking up kids, or taking kids to activities, etc. Both sites' calendars display which needs have been covered and which are open and need a volunteer.

■ Establish a reasonable schedule. Twice a week turned out to be best for us. Every day deliveries will overwhelm many families with more food than they can eat. Others may need that much. Tailor it to the family's needs.

■ Get some general guidelines on likes and dislikes, allergies, etc., then have each person decide what to deliver. A call to the caregiver to ask what the patient feels like eating that day is well-intentioned but is yet another call the caregiver has to answer and deal with. It also puts the burden on the caregiver to decide what to ask you to bring, wondering if it will be easy and convenient for you.

- Deliver small portions. If you want the family to have more to eat another day, put extra helpings in small freezable portions. Mark the frozen or freezable portions, identifying what it is, how to cook it, and the date when you prepared it.

- Deliver food in containers that do not have to be washed and returned, and make clear you do not want them returned.

- Comfort food is great, but mix it up. We all love comfort food in times of stress. But sometimes one more chicken and rice casserole is too much to bear. A nice salad can be truly welcome.

- If the patient is in the hospital, encourage the caregiver to get out for a meal. If she needs to stay close by, offer to eat with her in the cafeteria, or take a nice meal for her to the room.

- Make it abundantly easy for the family, and make clear it is easy for you. The call saying "I'm on my way to the market, what can I pick up for you" is lovely.

"It is the greatest of all mistakes to do nothing because you can only do little — do what you can."

— SYDNEY SMITH

CHAPTER 8

A Light Bulb Moment

O NE DAY **I** WAS AT HOME FOR A QUICK SHOWER when Ann was still in the hospital following her surgery. I turned on the lights in the bathroom only to have all three bulbs over the mirror go out at that moment.

It was the last straw that day. I simply could not cope with cancer *and* light bulbs. I took one of the burned-out bulbs and asked a friend to pick up three bulbs of that size for me. She looked a little puzzled. I said, "Don't ask. I just can't deal with burned out light bulbs right now." She gladly replaced them for me.

Sometimes the simplest errand can be too much when you are juggling so many glass balls and are facing such overwhelming stresses. When I told other friends the light bulb story they said, "Put me on the light bulb list. I'm happy to run errands."

A colleague at work stopped me in the hall one day and said, "I thought about you yesterday because I got the oil changed in my car. I realized that doing things like that may be tough for you. I'd be happy to take your car in to get the oil changed or anything like that." I never took him up on it, but it was very thoughtful of him to ask.

Dare I say, it was more helpful than his saying, "If there's anything I can do…."

"There are no little things.
'Little things' are the
hinges of the universe."
— FANNY FERN

LESSONS LEARNED

- Offer to run simple errands.
    - Pick up light bulbs.
    - Get a new battery for a watch.
    - Take the car to get the oil changed.
    - Pick up prescriptions.
    You get the idea.

- Don't be surprised or hurt if no one takes you up on it. Your offer lets them know you are thinking about them and want to help.

"Come again when you can't stay so long."

— WALTER SICKERT

CHAPTER 9

Visits May Be Welcome, Or Not

VISITS AT THE HOSPITAL or at home are sometimes marvelous for both the patient and caregiver. A visit can be a wonderful break, a supportive reminder of how much you care, and often a laugh or cry that everyone needed.

I remember vividly the friend who showed up with a cup of coffee and a smile on her way to work, the friend who showed up to sit with Ann at the hospital when we didn't know that we needed him, the friend who gave me a shoulder to cry on when I didn't even know I needed to cry. I have many memories of wonderful visits like that, most of which were unexpected.

There are times, of course, when a visit is not welcome. I won't go into unpleasant clinical detail, but you can imagine that there are times when a visit from even the closest friend would be awkward for everyone.

Even if things are stable, physical and emotional energy are both exceedingly limited. When you visit, the patient will often rise to the occasion and be so energetic and animated that you think she is having a great time and wants the visit to last as long as you can stay. In fact, even though she may be enjoying your visit, it is probably exhausting for her. I remember one friend visiting Ann in the hospital after her surgery. I was as glad to have the company as Ann was. I thoroughly enjoyed the visit, and it appeared that Ann did too. When the friend left, Ann turned to me and said, "Don't ever let anyone stay that long again."

The patient and caregiver may not have the heart to tell you it isn't a good time to visit or that it is time to wrap up the visit. Use your best judgment, and look for clues. Does the caregiver look harried? Does the patient look exhausted? Or do they look genuinely delighted to see you — in their eyes, not in what they say? If the caregiver stands up and says "thank you for stopping by," that's a good sign that it would be best to leave. Again, even if the patient appears to be enjoying the visit, the caregiver may be able to read the patient better, or may have been asked by the patient to keep the visit short. In any event, trust the caregiver's signals and understand that your visit is appreciated.

NOTE TO PATIENTS AND CAREGIVERS

The patient will often rely on you, the caregiver, to "control the traffic" – turning people away if necessary and keeping visits to a length that is manageable for the patient. Many visitors will have a difficult time knowing whether a visit is appropriate and, if so, how long of a visit will be okay. The patient may be able to let you know in advance whose visit and/or what length of visit may be welcome.

Gail Godwin's central character in *The Good Husband* is dying of cancer. She has many visitors during the winter, and she establishes a code with her husband to let him know when she is ready to end the visit. Her husband starts a fire in the room where she sees guests. Occasionally, he checks on her and asks if he should put another log on the fire. If she replies "yes," that is a signal that she wants to continue the visit. If she says, "I think we'll just let it burn itself out," that means she is ready to end this visit. Her husband then returns a few minutes later and announces it is time for her to rest.[1] You may want to set up a system to allow the patient to signal you if it is time to wrap up the visit.

[1] *The Good Husband,* Gail Godwin (Random House, 1994)

LESSONS LEARNED

- Do not call to ask if a visit would be welcome. In case you haven't picked up on it yet, I usually found telephone calls to be added stresses. There are exceptions of course, many of which I have already discussed. But calling to ask if a visit would be okay is problematic, because so much depends on the timing. Unless the caregiver is in a position to say categorically that the patient wants no visitors, it will depend entirely on what is happening and how she feels at the moment you get there. It is completely unpredictable.

- Just show up, but be prepared not to visit if it is not a good time.

- Keep it short. Even if the patient and caregiver seem to be enjoying your visit, keep it short. If they want you to stay longer, they will let you know. Be attuned to signals. If they say, "Thank you for coming by," that is a signal that it is time to go.

"My evening visitors, if they cannot see the clock, should find the time in my face."
— RALPH WALDO EMERSON

"At my age
flowers scare me."
— GEORGE BURNS

CHAPTER 10

"Flowers Feed The Soul."[3] Then Again…

THE AFTERNOON ANN AND I MET with the gastroenterologist who spelled out the likely implications of her tumor, we stopped by a market to pick up a few things. In the midst of my daze, I saw some pretty flowers and asked Ann if she would like for me to get her some. She replied, "I'm not dead yet."

Please do not take this to mean that flowers are never welcome. They can be uplifting and cheerful and just the right touch. There were many times when flowers brought a big smile to Ann's face and brightened her room. Sometimes a small bunch of flowers from someone's garden would show up on our front porch, with or without a short note. Those were always welcome.

But too many flowers can have the opposite effect. It can be depressing. We went to visit a friend shortly after he was diagnosed with cancer, and his house was full of big floral arrangements. His wife said, "It looks like a funeral parlor in here."

[3] The Koran

Hospital rooms are small and have little shelf space. Some floral arrangements were too big to put anywhere in the hospital room.

Another problem we encountered was that Ann was sensitive to strong smells when she was in the hospital. I had to take some beautiful flower arrangements home because the smell was overwhelming to her.

Chemotherapy also often makes patients unusually sensitive to smells. Be aware of that, and avoid sending flowers (or foods) with strong scents.

"Yet do much less, so much less…Well, less is more."

— Robert Browning
(Andrea del Sarto)

LESSONS LEARNED

- Flowers sent to a hospital room are most welcome if the arrangement is small and the scents are not strong.

- Plants are most welcome if they do not have to be replanted (yet another thing on the "to do list").

- Too many floral arrangements at once can be overwhelming — emotionally and practically. If it seems like an obvious time to send flowers, many others may be having the same thought. A small arrangement at an odd time may be just the right cheer.

- A big, formal arrangement may seem too reminiscent of a funeral parlor. Sometimes smaller, picked from the garden, or kept in a simple arrangement is just the right touch.

"*Apprehension, uncertainty, waiting, expectation, fear of surprise, do a patient more harm than any exertion.*"

— Florence Nightingale

CHAPTER 11

A Routine Game of Russian Roulette

HELOISE'S HUSBAND JOHN had a brain tumor. Like most cancer patients, he went in for scans periodically to check on the status. A friend went with them one day and remarked, "This must seem routine to the two of you by now."

Heloise replied: "Like a routine game of Russian Roulette."

Cancer patients' experiences are unique to each patient in many ways, but every cancer patient I have ever met will tell you that one of the worst things about the whole experience of cancer is waiting for the results of each scan. That was certainly true for me and for Ann. I usually felt nauseated for about a week before each scan and until we got the news. Our news was often good — Ann had many "clean" scans that showed no evidence of cancer. Those reports were moments of unmitigated joy for me. I shouted it from the rooftops (virtually at least, through e-mails and on CaringBridge). Other reports were not good. But universally, waiting for the results was a deeply anxious time.

"As a rule, what is out of sight disturbs men's minds more seriously than what they see."
— Julius Caesar

LESSONS LEARNED

- Know that waiting for results of scans is a deeply anxious time for the patient and caregiver. There is nothing you can "do" about this other than to recognize and acknowledge what a stressful time it is.

- Do not minimize the reality of how anxious this time is. It is not helpful for friends to say "I'm sure it will be fine," or "Don't worry. I know the scan will be clean." You don't know that, and it sends the message that the patient is wrong to be anxious — not living up to your expectations that they be upbeat and positive.

"Who takes the child by the hand takes the mother by the heart."

— DANISH PROVERB

CHAPTER 12

It Takes A Village

HILLARY **C**LINTON HAS FAMOUSLY said "It takes a village to raise a child." It can be especially true when one of the child's parents is critically ill and the other is an overwhelmed and overwrought caregiver.

I know of a young mother whose husband has colon cancer. Chemotherapy, doctor visits, scans, support group…How do you juggle all of that with work and play dates and getting dinner on the table? Her friends offered to keep the children, but her children didn't know many of her friends. She didn't want the kids to be shuttled from one stranger to the next. She also faced repeated explanations of bed time routines, food allergies, and which stuffed animals must be within arm's reach at all times.

Her friends came up with a solution. They started a baby-sitting fund, which allows the parents to hire sitters who know their children and their routines. Familiar baby-sitters also give the children some stability, which is needed when family life has been turned upside down.

If you know the patient's children, and they are comfortable with you, by all means offer to pick them up from school, drive them to piano or soccer, or feed them and get them to bed. Offer to do whatever you can do for the children with reasonable effort, but, as with everything you offer, understand if the patient or caregiver doesn't take you up on it.

Websites can help coordinate taking care of children and their activities. For example, lotsahelpinghands.com has a calendar that shows family activities and needs for each day — babysitting, rides to soccer practice or piano lessons, carpool pickup, and the like. It also shows when meals are needed. Volunteers can sign up to take care of certain tasks. The calendar shows which needs are taken care of and which still need volunteers. The patient and caregiver can log on and know who is helping with what on a given day. Confidence that children are taken care of helps relieve pressure for everyone.

LESSONS LEARNED

- Offer to take care of the children — pick them up from school, take them to piano lessons, feed them, put them to bed, whatever they need.

- Set up a baby-sitting fund to allow the parents to hire sitters who know the children and their routines.

- Set up a web site at lotsahelpinghands.com or a similar site that coordinates care for children, meals, and other family needs.

"I dislike helplessness in others and in myself, and this is by far my greatest fear of illness."

— JOHN STEINBECK[1]

[1] Travels With Charley (1962)

CHAPTER 13

To Do Or Not To Do

A **FRIEND TOLD US A STORY** about her friend Scott, who was weak from chemotherapy treatments. His partner was accustomed to taking care of everything and was happy to do it. At lunch time, he headed to the kitchen and found Scott getting things out to make sandwiches. His partner said, "I'll make lunch. Go sit down and rest."

Scott was livid: "I can make a sandwich!"

This is a delicate line for caregivers and friends to walk — the line between letting the patient do what he can do for himself and taking care of him when he needs it. This line also moves unpredictably. Something the patient wanted help with yesterday may be something he wants to do himself today. It may have changed because of how the patient feels physically or emotionally today. Today may be a day when the patient is lamenting how much autonomy he has lost. The patient may be frustrated that he can no longer take care of his family. On the other hand, today may be a day when the patient feels weak and has no energy to do anything.

The patient may also want to set boundaries around what friends do or see. Ann didn't want friends to see her throw up or double over in pain. My friend Jan's neighbor, Lynn, was in late stages of metastasized breast cancer when Jan offered to do her laundry. Lynn begged her not to. Even though Jan had helped her with laundry and other things around the house when Lynn was healthy (and busy), Lynn didn't want friends to do laundry now that she was sick. Patients often want to maintain friends as friends, rather than see them as caregivers.

It is hard, if not impossible, to get this right every time. The patient will not always tell you until you have already done or said the "wrong thing."

Just be aware that this is a sensitive issue for patients. Do the best you can to be attuned to what and how much the patient wants to do and can do for himself. Realize that you will not always get it right, and roll with the punches as best as you can. When the patient is able to do something for himself, let go of your need to take care of everything. It doesn't matter whether the patient is able to do something "right" or as well as he once did. Give him the gift of letting life seem as normal as possible.

LESSONS LEARNED

■ Be aware that the patient may want to do things for himself, but may not, and that may change with no warning or predictability.

■ Let the patient set the boundaries, within reason, on how much help he gets and who provides the help. Needless to say, sometimes the patient does not know or is resistant to what truly needs to be done. You must of course use appropriate judgment. But if circumstances allow, give the patient as much independence and control as you can.

"We are masters of the unsaid words, but slaves of those we let slip out."
— WINSTON CHURCHILL

CHAPTER 14

"If You're Inclined to Say This, Don't"

ANN JONES WAS an unusually open and direct person, even when she was in the best of health. At the end of her life Ann sometimes went beyond direct. She lost some of the filter we all — even Ann — use to keep conversation polite.

Shortly before she died, when a friend got up to leave after a brief visit, Ann said: "If you're inclined to come again, don't." (Fortunately, the friend understood completely.)

I have paraphrased this directive from Ann to introduce a tricky but important subject: What to say, or not say, to cancer patients, as well as their caregivers and families. This is a tough subject for many reasons:

- *Every situation is unique.* Cancer, cancer treatments, and the entire experience are intensely individualized experiences.

- *Cancer changes everything.* The person you knew who now has cancer may be a different person in many ways. The strong, self-confident person likely now feels at a loss and out of control. The person who would have never darkened the door of a support group may now crave that support. When Ann first started going to a support group, her daughter said, "I never thought of you as a support group type of person." Ann's reaction was, "I never was a cancer patient type of person." That, of course, had changed.

- *The situation, and how the person feels at any given moment, changes constantly.* At any given moment, the patient or her caregiver or her family may want to laugh or cry; talk about how they feel or not; talk about details of the treatments and so-called side effects[3] or not; and do things for themselves or not. For Ann and me, many days, weeks, and months were a mixture of hope and despair, balanced in different ways by each of us depending in part on the circumstances of the moment, in part on our own natures and outlooks, and in part on how we happened to be feeling at the moment.

- *Things change constantly, but the change is not linear.* Life with cancer is more like a roller coaster than

---

[3] So-called "side effects" are anything but "side effects." Many effects from treatments become central and all-consuming. Sometimes the "side effects" are more debilitating than the cancer and even more deadly, at least more quickly, than the cancer. Surgery to remove a spinal tumor may leave you paralyzed. Chemotherapy may damage other organs. Vomiting, nausea, rashes that make it too painful to lay your head on a pillow, intense fatigue that makes it impossible to get out of bed or to walk 10 yards...The list is endless.

a straight drive from point A to point B. You may think that things are "progressing," such that once the patient makes a decision or goes through a certain phase, his thoughts or feelings will progress forward in a linear fashion to adapt to the new reality. That would be logical, but cancer is not logical. Emotions are not logical. Thoughts and emotions go back and forth, up and down, two steps forward and one step back.

Given this emotional minefield, what should you say to a cancer patient, his caregiver, or his family members?

I cannot give you any absolutes here. I can tell you, however, a number of examples of things people tend to say that cancer patients, their caregivers, and their families almost universally find unhelpful if not hurtful. People who say these things undoubtedly have the best intentions and are well-meaning. It would not have occurred to me before Ann had cancer that some of these remarks would be problematic. But they are. Before reading this list, take heart. The next chapter gives you some suggestions on thing you *can* say or do that are more likely to hit the mark.

Now for the hit parade of things often said but rarely helpful:

- **"You are so strong." or "You are one of the strongest people I know."** People who are fighting cancer, a debilitating illness, or serious injuries from an accident do not feel strong. Saying "you are so strong" only reminds them that they are not strong at the moment, or makes them feel that they are not living up to expectations that they be strong. It can send a signal that they need to appear strong when they are around you, which means they can't be true to who they are or what they are feeling or what they are going through at the moment. They need to know that it is okay not to be strong. It is okay to rely on others for help. It is okay to feel weak.

A note in Ann's CaringBridge guestbook said: "Your illness shocks me because I always thought of you as such a strong, stalwart individual who shapes life as she wants it." This person undoubtedly meant this as a compliment. I feel certain she did not mean to suggest that if Ann had just been her strong self who managed her life beautifully she would not have gotten cancer. How easy it is to intend a compliment and have the opposite impact.

- **"You look so good."** This is a natural reaction when you see someone who you know has cancer or is going through treatments. We all have visual images of patients being emaciated, pale, bald or balding. If they look good when we see them we are quick to say: "You look good." Normally, people love to hear they look good. So how could this be problematic?

Again, cancer changes everything. This is a very sensitive issue for cancer patients. Saying "you look good" minimizes what's actually going on. It sends a positive, strong message to the patient, which they can't live up to or match. On the other hand, the patient may think "what did you expect? I'm not dead yet." It is very hard to win with this remark.

■ **"Be sure to stay positive"** or **"A good attitude is key."** We want our friends to stay positive and do everything they can, emotionally and physically, to beat the disease. Unfortunately, this sets the patient up for failure. If the cancer progresses, the patient must be at fault because she didn't have a good enough attitude or stay positive enough. Along with the "you are so strong" comment, asking the patient to stay positive also sends the message that the patient must be positive when she is around you and cannot be who she really is or true to what she is feeling at the moment.

■ **"The treatments are all over. You must be so relieved/happy."** This seems like a no-brainer. Of course everyone is relieved to be finished with treatments — right? Surprisingly, cancer patients often feel sad when treatments are over. This reaction surprises them as much as anyone, but it happens more often than you would think. Physically, it is wonderful to be finished with debilitating treatments. Emotionally, it may be another matter altogether. The treatments may have been horrible, but treatments at least represented doing something tangible to fight the cancer. Moreover, the treatments were the focus for a long time. The patient's (and caregiver's) days and weeks revolved around treatments and recuperating from treatments. That set the pattern for life. When treatments end the patient must move into a new phase, a new uncharted territory. The "sword" of active or metastasized cancer is always dangling, and the fear of it ripping life apart again is never far from mind and heart. Did the treatments work? Was it worth all of the debilitating side effects? What happens next?

- **"It's only hair. It will grow back."** Many people who have never lost their hair have this reaction to a chemo patient losing his or her hair. If you are tempted to say this, don't. If you are thinking this, think again. Losing hair is devastating. First, having your hair fall out in chunks in your brush or in the shower is a crushing reminder: "I have cancer. I am so sick and full of poison I can't even keep hair on my head." Second, a bald woman looks sick. Whether she is seen bald or wearing a wig, hat, or scarf, she feels as if she is wearing a neon sign that says, "I have cancer." It feels like being naked in public. A bald head is another jolting reminder that life is no longer normal.

  Men face an even more dismissive attitude — "men can be bald" or "men look good bald." True, but how many men really *want* to be bald? Would there be a Hair Club for Men or countless hair loss treatments if men really didn't mind being bald? For those men who shave their heads because they truly want to be bald, it is their choice. Going bald with no control over it is a completely different matter.

- **"We are all dying…I could die on the way home from work today."** This remark dismisses what the cancer patient truly faces. This sends the message to the cancer patient that she is not facing anything worse or different from what everyone faces every day, which is of course not true. It also sends the message that you don't want to hear about the disease or the patient's fears.

- **"Chemo brain? Sounds like me. I forget things all the time, and I haven't even had chemo."** Many chemotherapy patients experience cognitive issues — trouble tracking conversations or books or movies, short term memory problems, and disorientation. It is frustrating and embarrassing. Patients call it "chemo brain." When we described Ann's struggles with chemo brain, many people laughed it off by saying something like, "Don't worry. We all do that." I feel certain these folks are trying to put the patient at ease and reassure her not to be embarrassed about it. But this type of response is dismissive and minimizes a terrible "side effect" of the chemo treatments.

■ **"I wonder how you got cancer."** This remark may seem innocuous and even supportive, but the real message it sends is: *"What did you do to cause this?"* Similar comments to the patient, or about the patient when talking to others, include:

— "Did you smoke?"

—"He was always under too much stress. He didn't know how to slow down."

— "She never got enough exercise."

Here is the sad reality: Marathon runners die of cancer. People who exercise every day die of cancer. Yoga experts die of cancer. Vegans die of cancer. Monks who pray without ceasing die of cancer. It is an equal opportunity destroyer. Cancer does not restrict itself to those who have unhealthy lifestyles or eating habits. Counselors spend a lot of time picking up the pieces when people who have cancer feel guilty, as if it were their fault.

As Forrest Church so aptly observed in his book *Love & Death*, "When we die, however we may have lived, the ultimate culprit is not sin or squalor. The culprit is life. Life draws death in its glorious train."[4]

■ **"My uncle had the same cancer. He had a lot of pain when he was dying."** I do not know what prompts people to say things like "I know someone who had the same cancer. It was horribly painful and he died

---

[4] Love & Death, Forrest Church (Beacon Press Books, 2008)

within months." Likely, this is an immediate, unfiltered reaction. When someone hears about cancer it reminds them of someone they knew and they blurt out something about that person's experience with cancer. Or maybe they think it will show the patient that they empathize and understand how horrible and terrifying

cancer in general or a particular cancer can be. Whatever motivates it — don't say it. Think about how it would sound to you if you had cancer. Do you really think it would be helpful to hear about someone who had the same cancer who had excruciating pain, suffered through horrible treatments, and died? Keep this one to yourself.

- **"If you believe in God everything will be fine." Or "God only gives us as much as we can bear."** This remark, not unlike the remark about having a positive attitude, sets the patient up for failure. If the cancer progresses, does that mean the patient's faith is not strong enough? If the disease and treatments feel overwhelming and unbearable, does that mean the patient or caregiver doesn't trust God? If the person is not religious, does that mean he has cancer because he doesn't believe in God?

An insightful priest I know has written, "I am not comforted by the idea that God's help comes by means of being certain that I remain one straw short of snapping beneath the weight of my burdens. I need a God who can do more than just hold back the last straw."[5]

- **"You will be fine!"** or **"Don't worry, it was caught early."** We are all so uncomfortable with disease and death we are quick to focus on the positive or at least want to make the patient feel positive. We don't want to think about, let alone talk about, the terrifying possibilities. "You will be fine" or "Don't worry" is easy to say, but no one can know. No one can guarantee a good outcome, no matter how early it was caught or what the statistics show. These remarks also minimize the patient's fear and send him the message that you don't want to hear about his fear or concern.

- **"That's a good cancer to have if you have to have cancer."** I know of a young man with Hodgkin's Lymphoma. His friends told him this was a "good cancer" to have. He endured aggressive, relentless treatments.

---

[5] The Rev. Lisa Saunders, *The Blessing of a Ginkgo Tree: A Collection of Devotions by the Clergy of Christ Episcopal Church* (AuthorHouse, 2010)

The chemotherapy hammered him, causing vomiting and debilitating fatigue. He asked himself occasionally, while completely wiped out from treatments: "Is this the good part (of this "good cancer")?"

■ **"You should call my doctor. He has just the right treatment for you."** *or* **"I found this great remedy on the internet."** *or* **"I've heard this course you are following is not the best approach."** We all want to help, and most of us have our own experiences or know family members or friends with health issues. We may have some ideas about treatments that could work. We may also have heard something negative about the course the patient has chosen. These are not appropriate topics for conversation, however.

I know a patient whose doctor had decided it would enhance her quality of life for her to have a feeding tube to continue getting nutrition, even though she was in a very late stage of her disease. Several friends commented that nutrition for her at that point was also "feeding the cancer." That may have been true, but she and her doctor had considered all of the ramifications carefully and had chosen that route. It was not helpful for friends to question the decision.

It is almost never helpful to tell stories about your own experiences or offer advice on the health issues. Every experience is different, and you may not know all of the factors that impact decisions for this patient. The patient and caregiver may well feel overwhelmed by options already. Hearing your ideas may add to the confusion. If the patient or caregiver wants your input on treatment options, they will ask you. If they don't ask, don't offer these suggestions.

- **"I would just sit around and plan his funeral."** Our friend John chose to get treatment for his head and neck cancer at a medical center out of town. His wife Wendy went with him on many trips but not every trip. One of her friends asked her what she did when John was away getting treatments. Wendy said, "I manage to keep myself busy." Her friend said, "I would just sit around planning his funeral." Perhaps this person admired Wendy for not dwelling on the worst possible outcome. Perhaps she just blurted this out without thinking. Whatever prompted this comment, it is not helpful to assume the worst.

- **"Tell her I'm thinking about her."** People said this to me all the time. I wanted to say "Why don't *you* tell her?" I was happy to tell Ann people were thinking about her, and she appreciated hearing that. But it was much more meaningful for her to hear directly from people who cared. So when you catch yourself saying "Tell her I'm thinking about her," follow it up by sending a card or note or e-mail or flowers, or put a note on the CaringBridge website — something to let the person know directly that you are thinking about her.

- **"I hate to remind you about it."** You may hesitate to say anything about the diagnosis or treatments for fear of reminding the patient or caregiver about it. Trust me, you will not be reminding them of something they are not already thinking about.

Barbara Kingsolver captured this reality when she wrote about a character whose husband had recently died: "It took so much energy to keep Cole outside her thoughts for a single minute. And yet people still said, 'I didn't want to remind you.'"[6]

The patient and caregiver are constantly thinking about some aspect of the disease or treatment. If you say nothing to acknowledge it, the patient or caregiver will likely wonder if you don't know about it, or don't care, or are just too uncomfortable to talk about it.

Some friends apparently decided they did not want to remind us of Ann's cancer when they were with us. Sometimes the subject never came up, even during a lengthy meal or leisurely time with friends who knew all about the cancer. Ann would often say to me on the way home: "They didn't say one word to me about my cancer." She didn't want to dwell on it, but she wanted people to acknowledge it and give her a chance to talk about it if she wanted to.

[6] *Prodigal Summer,* Barbara Kingsolver (HarperCollins, 2000)

■ **"No matter what, you have to keep fighting."**
and, like unto it: **"Battle with cancer."** We all want
to cling to the hope that cancer can be beaten. As
long as someone is undergoing treatment, there is
a chance. We want the patient to have a "fighting
attitude" (very much like the "positive attitude"). But
we need to let the patient decide on her own when
and how to fight cancer. The patient doesn't need
to live up to other people's expectations about what
treatments to seek and how long to seek treatments.

I know a patient who was considering not having
radiation treatments. Her daughter said: "Mom,
that's so selfish of you. You have to take every
possible treatment." Her mother replied: "So I have
cancer but it's really all about you?"

It is hard to accept the point when no treatments
can be effective, or when the patient chooses quality
of life over more treatments. We need to recognize
that acceptance is not "giving up." It is not "losing
the battle with cancer." It is accepting reality and
making the most of life — whatever life is left.

Almost every cancer patient I know hates the
terminology "battle with cancer." Again, it sets the
patient up for failure. It implies that if he can just
fight hard enough or have the right "battle plan,"
he should "win." If he dies, people so often say
"He lost a long battle with cancer." Ann hated that
terminology and insisted that her obituary not say
anything of the sort. I agree.

In my view, Ann defeated cancer and left it in the dust. She maintained extraordinary strength and grace. She faced the diagnosis, the horrible treatments, and the ultimate reality of her death with her classic directness and openness. With her eyes wide open and head up, she took all cancer had to dish out and continued to live her life. She spent time with people she loved, and she let them know it. In the end, she left cancer behind as she moved on to a more glorious life, free from any cancer or pain.

"A friend is someone who helps you up when you're down, and if they can't, they lie down beside you and listen."

— UNKNOWN

CHAPTER 15

So What *Can* I Say?

ONE MAY REASONABLY ASK, "What in the world *can* I say that won't be taken the wrong way?"

The first answer is that you don't need to be quick to say anything. Let the patient or caregiver talk. Let him tell his story, or as much of his story as he wants to tell. Let him set the tone. If he talks about movies or books, it probably means he doesn't want to talk about his health right now. If you cannot tell what mood he is in, ask. A friend who visited Karen in the months of recovery after the tree fell on her said, "I don't know whether to be upbeat or calm." She replied, "Be calm please, I'm tired today."

If the patient talks about his health or treatments or fears or feelings, you will be giving him a great gift by giving him an opportunity to do that. Just listen.

A little girl who was sent on an errand was late getting back. Her mother demanded an explanation. The girl explained that on her way to the store she saw a friend who was crying because her doll was broken.

Her mother said, "Oh, so you stopped to help her fix her doll."

"No," replied the girl; "I stopped to help her cry."[7]

We all want to say or do the right thing. We want to make things better. But often the best thing we can do for someone is to just listen, just be with them, just let them feel what they are feeling. Cancer and cancer treatments are scary and painful. There isn't much any of us can do to "fix" it. Saying something upbeat or "encouraging" may have the opposite result of diminishing what the patient or caregiver is feeling.

The other advantage of not being too quick to say something is that it gives you a chance to think about how it may come across. Many of the examples outlined in the last chapter are things that people tend to blurt out without thinking. With a moment's reflection, most of us would not tell someone who has just been diagnosed with pancreatic cancer about the painful and inevitable death of someone else we knew who had pancreatic cancer. Give it a little thought before you say the first thing that comes to mind. Saying nothing at all may be the best thing to do.

The most helpful things people said to me were questions that encouraged me to tell them how I was doing, what I was thinking, and what I was feeling. An e-mail asking "How is Ann? How are you?" often

[7] The Rev. Martha Hedgpeth, *The Blessing of a Ginkgo Tree: A Collection of Devotions by the Clergy of Christ Episcopal Church* (AuthorHouse, 2010)

prompted a lengthy journal-esque reply from me. I found it therapeutic to be able to just "talk." (I also kept those e-mails and now have a journal of sorts, even though I didn't take the time to write true journal entries at the time.)

Try open ended questions that let the patient or caregiver set the tone and tell you what is on their hearts and minds (or not, depending on what *they* want to talk about):

- "How is it going today?"
- "How are you feeling?" (The patient or caregiver can decide whether to talk about how he feels emotionally or physically.)
- "Tell me about it." (The patient or caregiver will tell you what "it" is.)

Other helpful remarks acknowledged the pain, the angst, the exhaustion. Consider saying something along these lines:

- "I am so sorry you have to go through this."
- "My heart goes out to you."
- "You must be exhausted."
- "I'm so sorry the treatments are so debilitating."
- "Waiting for scan results must be almost unbearable."
- "You must be on tenterhooks" (if the patient is in remission or waiting for test results).
- "I hope you can somehow find some peace in all of this."

- "You're not alone. Call me if you need to talk or vent or cry or if you just want me to come be with you."
- "You are juggling so much. Here's what I'd like to do to help" (then offer something specific).

"Love of our neighbor in all its fullness simply means being able to say to him, 'what are you going through?'"

— Simone Weil

LESSONS LEARNED

- Just listen. Let the patient or caregiver set the tone for the conversation, and listen to what he has to say.

- Don't try to "fix it." Just be there, listen, and share the suffering.

- Think before you say anything. How will it sound? If it could come across as dismissive of what the patient or caregiver is feeling, don't say it.

"What is without periods of rest will not endure."

— OVID

CHAPTER 16

"Take Care of Yourself."

PEOPLE OFTEN SAID TO ME, as the caregiver, "Take care of yourself." They were right, of course, that I needed to take care of myself and stay healthy in order to stay strong and take care of Ann, continue working when I could, take care of things around the house, etc.

My first reaction to this statement, however, was "How, exactly, am I supposed to do that?"

After all, I was at the hospital all day and night, or back and forth between the hospital and the Hospice House, and I needed to work, pay the bills, take care of the pets, get groceries, pick up prescriptions, deal with health benefits and doctors…the list seemed endless. The stress of what Ann was going through was almost unbearable in and of itself, even without all of the stresses of living day to day under the suddenly difficult circumstances.

If people who are close to you and close to the situation repeatedly tell you to take care of yourself, listen to them. They know you and love you and can see when you need a break, often before you can see it.

If you are a caregiver, be mindful of and attentive to the things you need to do to give yourself a break. What would be particularly relaxing for you? It may be taking a walk, writing in a journal, talking to a friend, watching a favorite television show, gardening, taking time to meditate. Be intentional about doing whatever you need to do to "stay sane" and give yourself a meaningful break.

There will always be something you could be doing, or feel you should be doing, for the patient or the household. But other people can do many of those things. Only you can be the spouse (or the daughter or the mother). This may well be a marathon, not a sprint. You need to pace yourself so that you can be there and play the crucial role that only you can play. Don't feel guilty about taking a break.

At one point when Ann had been in the hospital for weeks with a particularly distressing complication that was causing deep confusion and disorientation, I was virtually at the end of my rope. I had scheduled a massage to ease the tension that was wracking my body and soul. Things kept moving so unpredictably I worried I couldn't get away for my massage. Our support group counselor all but ordered me to get that massage. She knew that the world would not come to an end if I was away from Ann for an hour or so, and she knew how much I needed that break.

Instead of saying "take care of yourself," it is more helpful to offer to do something specific to take some of the burden off of the caregiver. Think of something that will be a true break for that specific person. Is retail therapy the best prescription? Will a game of golf be the best break imaginable? A few hours in the garden? A trip to the gym? A massage? A mani/pedi? A night at the old ball game? A morning at the office? The right answer will depend entirely on the specific person and what they truly enjoy.

For example, you can say "I want you to take care of yourself. May I sit with [the patient] to give you a chance to go to a movie, play golf, have a leisurely dinner…?" "Or may I take care of errands or things that need to be done around the house?"

Ann's yoga teacher offered several times to work with me, at no cost, to help me stay healthy and reduce the stress. My sister sent me a gift certificate for a massage. Those gifts were terrific ways to help me take care of myself.

My friend Laurie reports that her friends knew that working in her garden would be therapeutic for her in the midst of her husband's treatments. They tilled the soil and got it ready for her to plant to her heart's content. It was just the respite she needed.

LESSONS LEARNED

- Think of something that would be relaxing or a good "get away" for the caregiver (shopping? massage? yoga? gardening? golf?). Make it happen by giving a gift certificate, setting up an appointment, taking care of the preparations.

- Sit with the patient to allow the caregiver time for the break he needs.

- Run errands or take care of tasks to give the caregiver time for the break he needs.

"Prayers go up and blessings come down."

— YIDDISH PROVERB

CHAPTER 17

"You Are In My Thoughts And Prayers."

"YOU ARE IN MY THOUGHTS AND PRAYERS" is a remark heard often when people face critical illness, and it is appreciated. But I was particularly moved when a friend asked, "How can I pray for her?" She wanted to know specifically what Ann needed at the moment. At that moment I asked her to pray that Ann could eat enough and gain strength as she recovered from surgery so that she would be stronger going into chemotherapy. Later the focus of prayer was completely different.

Notes from friends sometimes included short prayers or passages from scripture. I found that helpful. Along the lines of asking "how can I pray for her," a specific prayer let me know not only that the friend was praying for us, but also let me know what he or she was praying.

My friend John tells a story about an offer of prayer that he found particularly helpful. John had recently finished treatments for head and neck cancer when someone asked him: "May I pray for you?"

When John replied, "Yes, thank you," the person added, "Let me know when I can take you off of my prayer list." This made clear that he indeed planned to pray for John, and he wanted to know when John was better.

Another friend who sat with me while Ann was in surgery pressed a small book into my hand as I was called to meet the surgeon. It was a copy of *Ministry to the Sick,* a publication of The Episcopal Church's Church Publishing Company. It has prayers and passages of scripture and daily devotions that are helpful in ministering to the sick. My friend knew that I was an Episcopalian who would appreciate this book. I kept it by my bedside throughout Ann's hospital stay and for the next four years. It was a comforting resource.

Prayer is intensely personal. Many people are uncomfortable with prayer or do not have a faith tradition that values prayer. I would never presume to suggest that anyone pray for anyone else. But if you want to pray for people who are critically ill, ask them how you can best pray for them. If (and only if) you know them well enough to know of a prayer book or book of readings they would find helpful, give them a copy.

LESSONS LEARNED

- Ask how you can pray for the patient or caregiver. What is the best focus of prayer at the moment?

- Send a copy of a prayer or short passage from scripture, or give them a copy of a prayer book or book of readings *if* you know the patient or caregiver well enough to be certain it will be well received.

"A real friend is like an angel who warms you with her presence and remembers you in her prayers."

— Unknown

"Constant use will not wear ragged the fabric of friendship."

— DOROTHY PARKER

CHAPTER 18

"Let's Get Together Sometime"

HOW OFTEN DO WE SAY "Let's get together sometime?" We have the best of intentions, but we often let months or even years go by without ever spending time with that person. We all do this. We laugh about it, dismissing it as part of "life in the fast lane." It took Ann's diagnosis to jolt us into the realization that life is too short. Literally. After her diagnosis, we began to be much more intentional about spending time with people we cared about.

One of our friends suggested a standing Thursday night dinner at a Chinese restaurant. No calling each other or planning ahead was required, unless someone couldn't make it. Otherwise, we just showed up. Even with busy and unpredictable schedules (not to mention unpredictable health), we managed to see each other at least two or three times a month, which was much more frequent than we had ever managed before. With other friends we made a point of getting lunch or dinner on the calendar, and we pulled out calendars at the end of the meal to plan the next one.

Regardless of your health and that of your family and friends, recognize how fragile life can be. Take the initiative to spend time with people you care about. Get it on the calendar. Then get the next one on the calendar. With any luck, you will all grow old together and have many memories to look back on. Whatever happens, you will not regret spending time with people you love.

"Spend the afternoon.
You can't take it with you."
— ANNIE DILLARD

LESSONS LEARNED

■ Take the initiative to schedule time with people you care about. Don't let yourself or them get by with just saying "let's get together sometime."

■ Schedule a standing "date" for dinner or lunch or just time together.

■ Schedule the next get-together before you leave this one.

"If a friend is in trouble, don't annoy him by asking if there is anything you can do. Think up something appropriate and do it."

— EDGAR WATSON HOWE

Conclusion

THE ANSWER TO THE QUESTION "Is there anything I can do?" is "yes." The key is to think of something you can and would like to do, something that you have the skill and time to do, and *just do it*. Don't force the patient and caregiver to make a decision. They are making so many decisions already — including potential life and death decisions. One more decision may be too much.

As with most of the suggestions I've made, there is no "one size fits all" magic answer. There may be a fine line between being helpful and being intrusive. Use your judgment. For example, leaving a card or treat on the porch is never too intrusive. A visit could be.

If you ever get a call from the patient or caregiver, regardless of how he or she sounds, know that there is likely desperation behind that call. Be prepared to drop what you are doing and answer the call — literally and figuratively. One of our friends instructed her assistant to interrupt her if Ann or I called, no matter what she was doing. Just knowing she had given that instruction was incredibly supportive to us.

Know that it always matters that *you* did something. It matters, more than you know, that *you* are there, that *you* showed up, that *you* offered, even if the patient or caregiver isn't up to seeing you or doesn't need what you have offered. Ann often didn't even want to hear the CaringBridge messages. She just wanted to know who had written. John was grateful to know a friend had shown up at the door, even though John was too weak to see him at the moment.

Just do it. You, the patient, and the caregiver will be so glad you did.

"Praise the bridge that carried you over."

— GEORGE COLMAN

"Thank You,
Thank You Very Much"[1]

I DEEPLY APPRECIATE THE MANY, many things people did to support Ann and me throughout the almost four years of her illness and the continuing support after she died. I tried valiantly to write thank you notes for meals and errands and flowers and all of the wonderful gestures. I did not manage to write everyone. If you are one of those people, please know how much I appreciate everything you did and forgive me for not writing at the time.

For those of you doing everything you can to support friends now, know that the patient and caregiver are overwhelmed. They are doing everything they can to keep putting one foot in front of the other. In the whirlwind of doctor's appointments and treatments and getting through the new adventures brought by each day, they may lose track of who has done what and who they have thanked. Forgive them if they don't write you a thank you note. Know that they appreciate what you have done and even that you

[1] Elvis

offered to do something. Most of all they appreciate that you care.

I am grateful to many who made this book a reality rather than a pipedream: My dear friend Susan McConnell, who read every draft and gave me great insights and illuminating stories from her own experience as a caregiver; our support group leader, Meg Turner, who has worked with cancer patients and their families for over 20 years and helped me understand how cancer patients may react to seemingly supportive statements; and John Munce, one of Ann's closest friends and someone I am now honored to call a friend, who gave me wise editorial comments and counsel on every aspect of this book, gave me input from his own experience as a cancer patient, and got feedback from some veterans of the cancer treatment world.

Special thanks to two terrific writing coaches/ editors: Peg Robarchek and Tommy Tomlinson. Your encouragement, comments, and edits were invaluable.

Finally, and most importantly, Ann Jones inspired me beyond my wildest dreams, in every aspect of my life. I could never have written this without her love and support, which I felt intensely when she was alive and continue to feel today. Thank you Ann. I love you.

Spell The End
of Cancer

ANN JONES LOVED SCRABBLE. She was good at it. She loved words, and she loved a challenge.

Our Scrabble set was well-travelled. It saw action by a lake in Montana, by a stream in the Canadian Rockies, overlooking snow-capped peaks in Switzerland, looking out at the ocean at Hilton Head Island, by the fire in a mountain cottage, in a B&B in Scotland, on the bow of a ship cruising around glaciers in Alaska, and on many flights to and fro.

After her diagnosis Ann loved focusing on Scrabble rather than pain, disease, chemotherapy, or anxious thoughts about what the future might hold. Scrabble was one of her reliable anti-anxiety "medications." Ann and I played many a game of Scrabble at 3:00 in the morning. When she was feeling better, we began playing Scrabble regularly with a group of friends. We never left the game without planning the next one.

Scrabble was also responsible for a mild panic one evening after work when I couldn't find Ann. We were scheduled to meet our Thursday night dinner buddies for dinner. I got home from work and found Ann's car, purse, and cell phone at the house, but no Ann. The dog was there, so she wasn't out walking the dog. I got more worried as more time went by. What if she went for a walk and lost her balance and fell, or was too weak to walk home? One of my dinner buddies drove me all around the neighborhood to look for her. Eventually we found her — across the street playing Scrabble. She had lost all track of time while playing Scrabble with our neighbor.

After Ann died, Scrabble came to mind as I began to plan a fundraiser for cancer research in her memory. Our Scrabble playing buddies came up with the name "Spell the End of Cancer" and helped me put it together.

In memory of Ann, and in hopes of ending this terrible disease (and eliminating many of the occasions for saying "if there's anything I can do"), a portion of the proceeds from sales of this book will be donated to cancer research and programs that support cancer patients and their families. This is one way I can "spell the end of cancer."

Summary of Lessons Learned

ABOVE ALL

- Do, or offer to do, something specific.
- Make it easy on the caregiver and patient, and make it easy on yourself.
- Offer something you are good at and is easy for you to do.
- Call on the way to the market or pharmacy to ask if you can pick something up for them.
- Take care of the details (meet the caregiver where it is convenient for her; deliver the meal to the patient's house; pick up the dog or the children or the dry cleaning...)

COMMUNICATION/TELEPHONE CALLS

- Let the patient and her family control the information flow; don't call them for updates.
- If the family hasn't set up a CaringBridge site or a similar web site, offer to do it for them. If they don't want to use a web site, offer to help set up a blog or send out e-mails or make calls to report updates to friends and family.
- Be sensitive to what the patient and her family are telling you, and be as supportive as you can while

acknowledging the gravity or difficulty of what the patient and her family are going through.

- The text of your message is less important sometimes than the fact that you reached out. A short message may be perfect. You don't have to be profound. Just be yourself.

- Avoid calling the patient or caregiver.

- If you can't refrain from calling, and you get voice mail, leave a short message so that the patient can hear your voice, but make clear that you don't need a call back.

- Unless you truly need a reply, make clear that you do not expect a reply to your e-mail or your call.

- If you want to contact the patient or family, use a card, a note, CaringBridge, an e-mail, or a text message — something that will not disturb them and that they can respond to when it suits them.

- If the patient or caregiver calls you, recognize the likely desperation behind the call, and be ready to listen and do whatever you can to help, right then.

PETS ARE WONDERFUL SUPPORT

- Does the patient have a dog or pet? Offer to take care of it, if you can, or find someone who can, while they are in the hospital. If they are home, offer to walk the dog, change the kitty litter, or pick up pet supplies — anything that lets the pet be a companion and not a burden.

- Do you have a dog that would be good around patients and hospitals? If so, volunteer to take your dog to visit patients. It is wonderfully uplifting for patients.

"TAKE A SEAT"/WAITING ROOMS

- If you think the caregiver would like company, offer to sit with her during surgery or lengthy procedures — or just show up, with a cup of coffee or just a smile.

- If the caregiver prefers not to have company, respect that. She may need that time for herself.

- Drop off a care package with puzzle books, pencils, and light reading the caregiver will enjoy.

FOOD

- Have a single point person coordinate meals, taking that burden off of the caregiver.

- Set up a web site at mealbaby.com or lotsahelpinghands.com or whatever new site may be even better. Both of these web sites include calendars. Mealbaby.com has a calendar showing when meals need to be delivered. Lotsahelpinghands.com has a calendar of activities and family needs, including meals or picking up kids, or taking kids to activities, etc. Both sites' calendars display which needs have been covered and which are open and need a volunteer.

- Establish a reasonable schedule. Twice a week turned out to be best for us for meals. Every day deliveries will overwhelm many families with more food than they can possibly eat. Others may need that much. Tailor it to the family's needs.

- Get some general guidelines on likes and dislikes, allergies, etc., then have each person decide what to deliver. A call to the caregiver to ask what the patient feels like eating that day is well-intentioned but is yet another call the caregiver has to answer and deal with. It also puts the burden on the caregiver to decide what to ask you to bring, wondering if it will be easy and convenient for you.

- Deliver small portions. If you want the family to have more to eat another day, put extra helpings in small freezable portions. Mark the frozen or freezable portions, identifying what it is, how to cook it, and the date when you prepared it.

- Deliver food in containers that do not have to be washed and returned, and make clear you do not want them returned.

- Comfort food is great, but mix it up. We all love comfort food in times of stress. But sometimes one more chicken and rice casserole is too much to bear. A nice salad can be truly welcome.

- If the patient is in the hospital, offer to take the caregiver out for a quick bite. If she truly needs to stay in the room or close by, take something good to eat to the room or offer to eat a meal with the caregiver in the hospital cafeteria. Company can be nice.

- Make it abundantly easy for the family, and make clear it is easy for you. The call saying "I'm on my way to the market, what can I pick up for you" is fabulous.

LIGHT BULB MOMENTS/SIMPLE ERRANDS

- Offer to run simple errands. Pick up light bulbs. Get a new battery for a watch. Take the car to get the oil changed. Pick up prescriptions. You get the idea.

- Offer to do the laundry, tend the garden, wash the dishes, take care of things around the house.
- Don't be surprised or hurt if no one takes you up on it. Your offer lets them know you are thinking about them and truly want to help.

VISITS

- Do not call to ask if a visit would be welcome. Unless the caregiver is in a position to say categorically that the patient wants no visitors, it will depend entirely on what is happening and how she feels at the moment you get there. It is completely unpredictable.
- Just show up, but be prepared not to visit if it is not a good time.
- Keep it short. Even if the patient and caregiver seem to be really enjoying your visit, keep it short. If they want you to stay longer, they will let you know. Be attuned to signals. If they say: "Thank you for coming by," that is a signal that it is time to go.

RUSSIAN ROULETTE/SCANS

- Know that waiting for results of scans is a deeply anxious time for the patient and caregiver. There is nothing you can "do" about this other than to recognize and acknowledge what a stressful time it is.
- Do not minimize the reality of how anxious this time is. It is not helpful for friends to say "I'm sure it will be fine," or "Don't worry. I know the scan will be clean."

You don't know that, and it sends the message that the patient is wrong to be anxious — not living up to your expectations that they be upbeat and positive.

IT TAKES A VILLAGE/CHILDREN

- Offer to take care of the children — pick them up from school, take them to piano lessons, feed them, put them to bed, whatever they need.
- Set up a baby-sitting fund to allow the parents to hire sitters who know the children and their routines.
- Set up a website at lotsahelpinghands.com or a similar site that coordinates care for children, meals, and other family needs.

IF YOU'RE INCLINED TO SAY THIS, DON'T

This is a tough topic, in part because every situation is unique, and individual patients may react differently to certain remarks. They may even react differently on different days. But the following list includes things that most cancer patients tend to find not helpful, for reasons explained in the text.

- "You are so strong." or "You are one of the strongest people I know."
- "You look so good."
- "Be sure to stay positive" or "A good attitude is key."
- "It's only hair. It will grow back."
- "We are all dying…I could die on the way home from work today."
- "Chemo brain? Sounds like me. I forget things all the time, and I haven't even had chemo."

- "The treatments are all over. You must be so relieved/happy."
- "I wonder how you got cancer."
- "My uncle had the same cancer. He had a lot of pain when he was dying."
- "If you believe in God everything will be fine," or "God only gives us as much as we can bear."
- "You will be fine!" or "Don't worry, it was caught early."
- "That's a good cancer to have if you have to have cancer."
- "You should call my doctor. He has just the right treatment for you," or "I found this great remedy on the internet," or "I've heard this course you are following is not the best approach."
- "I would just sit around and plan his funeral."
- "Tell her I'm thinking about her."
- "I hate to remind you about it."
- "No matter what, you have to keep fighting," and, like unto it: "Battle with cancer."

SO WHAT CAN I SAY

- Just listen. Let the patient set the tone for the conversation, and listen to what he has to say. Try:
  - "How is it going today?"
  - "How are you feeling?" (The patient or caregiver can decide whether to talk about how he feels emotionally or physically.)
  - "Tell me about it." (The patient or caregiver will tell you what "it" is.)

- Don't try to "fix it." Just be there, listen, and share the suffering.
- Think before you say anything. How will it sound? If it could come across as dismissive of what the patient is feeling, don't say it.
- Consider saying:
  - "I am so sorry you have to go through this."
  - "You must be exhausted."
  - "I'm so sorry the treatments are so debilitating."
  - "Waiting for scan results must be almost unbearable."
  - "You must be on tenterhooks" (if the patient is in remission or waiting for test results).
  - "My heart goes out to you."
  - "I hope you can somehow find some peace in all of this."
  - "You're not alone. Call me if you need to talk or vent or cry or if you just want me to come be with you."
  - "You are juggling so much. Here's what I'd like to do to help" (then offer something specific).

"TAKE CARE OF YOURSELF"/ THINGS YOU CAN DO FOR THE CAREGIVER

- Think of something that would be relaxing or a good "get away" for the caregiver (shopping? massage? yoga? gardening? golf?). Make it happen by giving a gift certificate, setting up an appointment, taking care of the preparations.

- Sit with the patient to allow the caregiver time for the break he needs.
- Run errands or take care of tasks to give the caregiver time for the break he needs.

"YOU'RE IN MY THOUGHTS AND PRAYERS"

- Ask how you can pray for the patient or caregiver. What is the best focus of prayer at the moment?
- Send a copy of a prayer or short passage from scripture or give the patient or caregiver a copy of a prayer book or book of readings *if* you know them well enough to be certain it will be well received.

"LET'S GET TOGETHER SOMETIME"

- Take the initiative to schedule time with people you care about. Don't let yourself or them get by with just saying "let's get together sometime."
- Schedule a standing "date" for dinner or lunch or just time together.
- Schedule the next get-together before you leave this one.

JOSEPHINE **H**ICKS lives in Charlotte, N.C. She practiced law as a litigator for 30 years before joining the staff of a faith-based nonprofit organization. Originally from Greenwood, South Carolina, she graduated from The University of the South (Sewanee) and Vanderbilt University Law School. Daughter and spouse of Episcopal priests, she is active in the Episcopal Church and in the Anglican Communion. This book is born of her experience as the primary caregiver for her partner during almost four years with pancreatic cancer. Following her partner's death, she founded Spell the End of Cancer, a Scrabble event to raise money for cancer research. In hopes of eliminating many of the occasions for saying "if there's anything I can do," part of the proceeds of this book's sales will be donated to cancer research.

Ann Brewster Jones and
Josephine H. Hicks in
Vancouver, Canada, January 2008.